ISBN 979-8-9897701-5-1

Text & photographs © Jeremy Fernando 2024
Mustard Oil, Garlic, Chilli © Saudamini Deo, 2023

Published by Hidden Hand Press
www.hiddenhandbooks.com

HIDDEN HAND PRESS

that one time my grand-aunt
tried to kill us all
&
some such tales

Jeremy Fernando

Saudamini Deo, *Mustard Oil, Garlic, Chili*, 2023

under the jaguar sun

A spice, a pepper, a condiment, a companion, I go by many names.

Accompanying me, coming through lips during my travels through time. Over lands, seas, on the backs of horses, boats, goats, people. Making stops in bazaars, markets, souks, brought by traders, alongside empires, finding many a home, stoves, meals, meeting many who would me take for their own.

Defining their dishes, kitchens, writing the stories of their cuisines through me. As if I had always been here.

My piquancy, though, recalling a time of moon, memory, and muchness. Of searing. Under the jaguar sun.

Reminding their tongues this berry-fruit can never be tamed.

*I write you an onomatopoeia, convulsion of language.
I'm not transmitting to you a story but just words that
live from sound.*

~ Clarice Lispector

moderato cantabile

Garlic

She woke up that morning with lashings in her head.

A word that had long clung to her, like picnics and the Famous Five. Back then, she imagined it was their exploits which drew her in, but as time rolled on, she knew, without ever quite realising, it were the spreads that were actually calling her name.

I miss George.

She longed to tell her, if I hurt you, I'll make wine from your tears. But Michael Hutchence had already sung it. Sometimes others say your words for you. I suppose I was never one for verse. She never thought she had anything to say, that she had to say anything. I really thought she would stay.

If only she'd call.

Reaching over to the still-made side of her bed, she remembers G loving it spread over toast, the grin on her face as the crunch was accompanied by an explosion of rich verdant freshness, teeth sinking in velvet oiliness, a little garlicky kiss afterwards. Maybe if I make it, she would dream a little dream of me. Not that she even realised G's love for it until finding it in a letter, one not even addressed to her.

And makes —
makes this very trace.

Hope is a dangerous thing for one to have.

It be pretty dreaming behind a rainy windowpane.

Pine Nuts, untoasted

First time we met, we were by a river, standing.

Both having scampered from a work gathering,
one of those things we were obliged to be at, at
least that's what I told her, having needed to find
a way to have her for an evening beside me.
Perhaps that was the problem, me plunging
headfirst. At that moment, everything seemed
fine: we were both standing there, standing by
peaceful waters.

Hands might have touched.

They certainly did later, tearing into a margherita.
Laughing with joint memories, ones that we
couldn't possibly have had, or yet known.
Mozzarella stretching linking stringing us along.
And the way she twirled her finger around the
thread between, until softly my lips she brushed.

Things, they attract each other.

She invited me for a midnight dip, in a river that
for an evening was ours. I just wanna dance with

you — she might have just been repeating Lana del Rey or every other pop song ever written I didn't really care. Perhaps that was the problem, me plunging headfirst.

~ Matt Berninger

By the time everything crumbled, we realised we were more alike than we'd liked.

Basil

All she had to do was combine.

Surely all her years of bringing people together,
she thought to herself as she placed her shopping
on the kitchen counter not just putting them in
the same space but also handling them guiding
them even at times leading them by their noses,
should have made her an old hand at this. How
difficult could this be.

Moreover, she had a pestle on her side —
usually she could only dream of having a mallet to
go along with the smile she had to endure
wearing.

The only thing being things, unlike people, things
keep their secrets.

*If the colour yellow runs out
with what will we make bread?*

~ Pablo Neruda

Parmigiano

She felt so relaxed she decided to put on a record.

Nel nome del Padre e del Figlio e dello Spirito Santo ... the words tumbled out of her with the first grind of the pestle, turning slowly along the sides of the mortar; always start with offering gratitude *cara*. She instinctively went to a phrase following her since she was a child, one she repeated almost meditatively whenever she was asking for something, for a kind of nourishment, any forgiveness, some moment of kindness. It never failed to remind her of father, and sons she never had.

She liked the fact that hidden within it lay echoes of *nom nom nom*, another sound from her youth, a sound from another childhood almost, a preferred sound if she were being honest.

She put on a record to get herself to relax.

Pecorino

Place the garlic in the mortar. Take the pestle in
your hand, hold snugly in your palm, start to
mash in slow swirling motions. Gently. You're not
trying to pound them into submission, she hears
Nonna's voice every time, you're trying to coax
their essence into emerging. Add a dash of salt to
help. To build, you always need a grain of earth.

Once the yellow of the sun reveals itself, set aside.

Enter pine nuts, stage left. Give them space, *mia
cara*, let them play, and for you they'll put on the
glow of *il terreno*.

Lift the earth from the bowl. Start laying *basilico*,
in small batches so you have time to know them.
As the mortar becomes lush with forest green,
gradually introduce them to the yellow and the
brown.

Piano piano.

Give them room *cara* to engender themselves,
passare da maschio a femmina, transform into a
basilica. *Piccola*, don't try to make it the way you
think it should be. Love it, and let it be.

Amo, volo ut sis.

And when you hear the whispers of angels
singing, remember *cara*, sometimes they appear to
take the form of gargoyles, but don't be fooled, *i
demoni sono solo cherubini affamati*, shower them
with yellows of fire and the Tuscan sun, and
always swirling, bathe *la miscela* in drizzles of
green around which this world builds itself.

Taste *cara*, keep tasting, listen with your tongue.

Add salt to taste.

Moderato cantabile.

It be pretty building layers behind a rainy
windowpane.

Olive Oil

Someone once told me marriage is a life-long feat of diplomacy; the most important things must not be discussed.

Probably why we never did so.

I suppose the only reasonable thing to do was trade her for ghosts, it seemed the moderate thing to do. Time has a wonderful way of sifting, drowning noise, leaving us with memories of times our voices were in accord, surrounding a plate, bowl, dish, nary a word between us, singingly almost — in silence.

Something about breaking eggs to make omelettes. I'm not sure I ever believed it despite it being true, maybe even because it were.

I walked out on G, thought it would be easier that way, the most important things must not be discussed. I may have well been right, told myself abandonment is a form of freedom.

Thankfully ghosts never quite go away, they sing me each time to my bowl. Maybe if I make it she will dream a little dream of me.

Hope is a dangerous thing for one to have.

It be pretty dreaming behind a rainy windowpane.

Sometimes the horrible thing about being a human being is that something — a bit of history, as it were — happens to you, and there is nothing you can do about it.

~ David Mitchell

Irony won't save you from anything; humour doesn't do anything at all. You can look at life ironically for years, maybe decades; there are people who seem to go through most of their lives seeing the funny side, but in the end, life always breaks your heart.

~ Michel Houellebecq

una tierra de la baldío … vislumbres fragmentarios

— para Candela del Vella —

el tesoro es romperse desde adentro, 2022

breeding lilacs out of the dead land, 2022

sintiendo el olor a tierra mojada, 2022

walls | green | walls

green
turquoise the walls
maybe be
let's though call them
green
so

green
that being said
after an hour many
with four walls staring
surrounding submerging you
them anything would too turn
green

anyone
too

green
stare too long into the abyss
too, and back it will
at you, maybe that too
be what we fear, that
it be nothing we see
but

green

that all we be
be walls

green

yes, we'll all be together
in the shade of the old oak tree
when we meet beneath the green,
green grass of home

~ joan baez

every fruit has its secrets, 2017

The eye is simply a recorder, without or without our will. Perhaps the same can be said of the heart.

~ Maggie Nelson

Tout est arrangé, fabriqué, artificiel, tout est mis en scène, rien n'est franc, ou, pour le dire autrement, tout est art ...

~ Milan Kundera

a story of a man
— for Maurice James Beins —

Handsome in pink he was, went around telling everyone that his dad was a pygmy did he. Having decided from rather early in life that most rules were tosh, that no one should ever dress in anything but blue shorts and flip-flops, his best friends were dogs and cats and birds, mostly as they never lie — tell you in no uncertain terms when they like you and when not did they, like he.

One day he was walking down the street swinging his hands like he always did. Smiling at everyone like he always did. Never stopping like he always did. Except that suddenly he paused — a certain someone smiled back at him. The young woman hardly spoke. *This way please* was all she seemed to say, truthfully it was more her fingertips tippy-tapping on the windowsill that said what she had wished to say, for no sound escaped her lips.

But luckily, Morse code he knew.

They tapped their way into a new life, and in between twirls, he would whisper in her ear.

And these tales she took, and weaved them into her famous pots of curry did she. This worked out very well, for he were a firm believer in eating only what you love, and she, in putting love into what you eat.

Rather fortuitously, love to eat they both did.

I hear they had a son, and he was the envy of many, as he grew up on plates filled with stories. *The finest ingredients they were*, said he. A taste of this curry once I did have, and the tales still tingle on my tongue. In them be laughter and life, peppered with a twist of Pimm's No 1 on ice.

As the man in pink would have said, *'tis stories that fill your belly and curry that warms your heart*. Get enough I never could, and followed my nose the other day did I: though, pin-point the source of this scent couldn't I, no matter how hard I tried, realised it was everywhere I went.

It seems that everyone who has eaten from this pot now shares these spiels — and are never starved of yarns.

Which is why I now be before you.

And if just for a little moment you would take a while, indulge, and call to mind a little tale you've been told.

Let it fill you, warm you, bring a little sunshine to you. And remember that it's all right to smile a little, chuckle a little, or hell, even laugh out loud.

For, late last night the man in pink strolled by and I told him I was going to tell his tale. And I asked if he would stop by and say *hi*, if only for a bit. He said he will, but it might be hard to wave; *my mother only gave me two hands — the right for the whiskey, the left for me smokes.*

But he wants to leave you just one more tale before he had to go. He smiled a little smile, whispered in my ear, *there ain't enough beer in heaven, you gotta drink it here on earth.*

If any of the stories is lacking in restraint, this is because of the nature of the story itself ... for no story is so unseemly as to prevent anyone from telling it, provided it is told in seemly language ...

~ Giovanni Boccaccio

whiter shade of pale, 2021

I never ever imagine anything clearly or literally when I write. It's an act of listening. I listen to something. I hear what I write. But I don't see. I don't imagine. And where it comes from, I don't know.

~ Jon Fosse

Indeed, one could even say that every book has a core, and it's precisely to gain distance from that core — to leave it unsaid and untouched while somehow bearing witness to it — that it was written. Claiming to grasp something that must remain unuttered means falling from the status of author-witness to assume instead the legal status of author-owner.

~ Giorgio Agamben

impossible conversations
— *for Marguerite Duras* —

As we are having this conversation, as I am
speaking with — perhaps, even to — you, as you
are listening to me, I wonder if it is even possible
to speak of death, not to mention speak to Death.

Herself. Himself. Itself?

For, even as we spend quite a lot of our time
telling tales of death, of deaths, about death,
about deaths that are not quite just deaths, we are
merely making utterances about death, perhaps
even describing deaths, but are never really quite
able to say what death is ;

let alone whom.

Which opens the question: does one speak of
death, or *the idea of death?*

Keeping in mind that death — or Death, if you
prefer proper nouns — remains beyond one, even
as (S)He is always already within one. One only
experiences death; and as far as I can tell, no one

has come back to tell us whom we face, what we are facing. Or, whom is facing one. And perhaps, in facing death one is always alone: even if (S)He is there. Even the Nazarene. All he did was: announce his resurrection, pronounce that *to conquer death, you only have to die.* But, he didn't bother to tell us exactly whom — or what — he conquered. Which, in itself, is no reason to doubt his words, his claim. Perhaps he did overcome the idea of death — and only left its, his, her, effects untouched. After all, the last I checked, people were still affected, still dying. For which I am — morbid, as it may sound — strangely thankful. That way, at least I know I'm speaking with you.

Or, at least the possibility of you.

But, *which* you?

For, one should try not to forget that everyone dies twice: once bodily; the other when one is forgotten. Which might also mean that there are two, there is more than one, you. That speaking with one involves the death of the other, all others. And that, since I am — or at least am attempting to be — speaking to Death, this means that even the un-dead death must also be dead. Thus, I can only be speaking with you in memory of you.

For, even as I call you Death, even as I personify you, my only access to you is through your name; I can only attempt to speak of you, to you, imaginatively. And here, one should bear in mind that imagination springs from memory: for, to imagine something, one has to have an inkling of it, one has to first know of it. But, of death, I know nothing except its effects. And yet, we continue to speak of death, I continue to speak of death, you continue to listen to me speak about death.

Thus, always speaking the unspeakable.

Or, perhaps: speaking of a memory that I have yet to have.

And, since death is quite possibly a memory to come — even if you have never left my side — perhaps then, the only way I can know of this is if I, we, have always already been dead. And are only

waiting for our bodies to catch up with this
memory, this memory of the unknown.

Perhaps, that is the only way I can be speaking of
death to you. Even as I know not what I am
speaking of.

By speaking of death as it speaks through me.
Speaking to you as you speak through me ...

        ... in an infinite conversation

If this were to ever become a monologue, I don't think it should be memorised and performed, as it were. But read — as if one had written a speech in preparation to speak, but then when reading it, reading as if seeing all of this for the first time.

I live my death in writing. It's the ultimate test: one expropriates oneself without knowing exactly who is being entrusted with what is left behind. Who is going to inherit, and how? Will there even be any heirs?

~ Jacques Derrida

*The definition of the human condition
is a mise-en-scene itself.*

~ Alfredo Jaar

There is something in his voice that I did not hear at that time, a clamor which perhaps could only be grasped when the language was not our own.

~ Christina Tudor-Sideri

Before you die, you're a bastard. After that, you're a fucking saint.

~ Maurice James Beins

that one time my grand-aunt tried to kill us all

II

whilst lying down just there seemingly fairly
relaxed no less nary a care in the world certainly
no indication of movement nor consciousness she
certainly wasn't reacting to anything or anyone
who was around her and there were plenty of us
of them ;

I'd like to think maybe hold on to the thought
even if it were only a possibility a glimmer that
there be some sort of discerning discernment
taking place the only ones who were nearly taken
along for the proverbial ride were us not them not
that these terms were mine was really more how
she used to think of them at least that's what I
recall her saying she'd never admit to it though I
suppose one of the benefits of her just lying there
being no right of response well one of the benefits
were I being honest to me at least ;

one has to take comfort try to take some comfort
in being take comfort in trying to be part of the
ones she tried to kill I suppose though if one were to
be fair *tried to kill* might have been overstating it a
touch *take with her* could be more appropriate
whether it ever be appropriate to take with to
appropriate being a quite entirely different
question ;

after all she was lying in a coffin and
attempted-murder seems to require a little too
much movement for one who was lying down who
was never the most nimble one would never have
mistaken her for a ninja then again that's the kind
of thing the best of ninjas would have you think
so maybe we just didn't see her move maybe we
never saw her nimble movements maybe when
you're dead you can move without moving die
without dying lie without lying ;

tell me lies
tell me sweet little lies
tell me lies
tell me tell me lies

~ Fleetwood Mac

who knows thought it's not as if any of us have
been there before then again everyone dies twice
once bodily another time when one is forgotten if
we're lucky in that sequence then again if one is
forgotten no one is there to learn from one's death
maybe that's how Thanatos keeps his secrets
sending the Keres to sprinkle the waters of Lethe
on those who already know ;

suppose it's no surprise we've never quite been
sure why nor can we nor will we ever be able to be
sure why it were so ;

moreover it be fairly impossible to fairly know to
know fairly to 'suss out with any fairness if the
one lying there is lying there is no point of
comparison without motion without movement ;

she were just there soundly sleeping if that be
even the word do we even have an adjective for
one lying in a coffin ;

peacefully is just so banal and really how the fuck
does one even know they know knowing my
grand-aunt she almost certainly would have been
bored shitless you know ;

might have well been trying to take us all out fer
shits and giggles benefits of being dead be there
being no one left to judge you after all you need a
body to be brought before the law ;

Ooooooooooooo,
Yeah !

~ Randy Savage

she was *were* really it is not a notion of the past
can never be relegated to a linear movement of
time but a truth-term *she were* the one who first
introduced me to the magical world of
professional wrestling, the one who brought me *à
le monde où l'on catche* ;

to the world of *catch* where we *catch as catch can*
where one not just takes what one can but
perhaps more importantly that it be one's
opponent who tells you even dictates to speaks to
one how they would be could be even should be
caught and if you didn't catch it you just weren't
listening hard enough ;

perhaps like when we don't hear what the dead
tell us ;

maybe her almost putting-us-down was my
grand-aunt's way of making us slow down for a bit
to remove ourselves from the world to let
ourselves be caught by our selves our own bodies
to not just slow down this is not some silly
mindfulness session we're not in California baby
but to lie down in almost-death ;

there were twenty four of us at her wake I still
recall it like it were yesterday come to think of it
all recollections might as well have taken place the
day before just a moment ago ;

right before the collect-call takes place there's
always a price to pay for calling back memories
and the ten of us who were afflicted were directly
related to her no one else *just you not them all* she
might say some privileges you just don't want who
ever said you'd like all the gifts you were given
gifts could well be *giftig* ;

lying on my bed feeling like I'd been hit by a
frog-splash off the top rope ;

half-catatonic not moving for days just lying there
mind wandering drifting reminiscing
remembering fondly somewhat eternally watching
awaiting anticipating *crying waiting hoping* in
Buddy Holly's voice no less while Jimmy Snuka
awaits standing balancing prancing playing up the
madding crowd aligning himself on the
turn-buckle perpendicular to my prone
almost-cadaver preparing to pull-off a Superfly
Splash ;

Ohhhhhhhh
What a rush!

~ The Road Warriors

repeated remembrances rushing through me
calling out to me in the stillness of a time that was
both mine and not mine what does it even mean
to say that one is *on time* or that you are *in time* for
something can one *stand on* time *be inside* time is it
even a thing and might it always be *out of joint*
adjoined to what oh god what I need is a joint ;

for remembrances to be remembered there has to
be repetition so the same thing in a different time
same same but different ;

remember me kept ringing in my head *but how*
maybe that was the conundrum Daddy H was
facing not just that Sonny Ham was scribbling in
his notepad jotting down a reminder to avenge
him so he could take-off to play hooky with wispy
O but that he would not be remembered in the
right way in the way that was proper to him that
he felt was appropriate to him ;

remember me how would she have liked to be
remembered there really is no way to know
certainly much too late to find out no wonder
séances are so popular ;

Call me (Call me) on the line
Call me, call me any, anytime
Call me (Call me) I'll arrive
You can call me any day or night
Call me

~ Blondie

and maybe *remember me* is a mantra to be
constantly repeated chanted repeatedly chanted in
the hope that how she would like to be
remembered would call out to me ;

when repeated enough repeated repeatedly
becomes a habit which inhabits my *habitus* ;

addiction ;

> *Je compare la plume à une seringue, et toujours je
> rêve d'une plume qui soit une seringue ...*
>
> ~ Jacques Derrida

Woooooo !

~ Ric Flair

;

a telephone

          ... ring ring

               .

               .

               .

              tone
              or
              pulse

               .

               .

               .

              or perhaps a bead
            atop half a boomerang

               .

               .

   .   .   .   .   .

   .

   .

through the looking glass
coming back at me

oh oh oh what a rush!

;

III

and as we wind on down the road,
our shadows taller than our soul, 2022

I

*History is always in danger of being a little altered or touched up
and brought closer to fiction ...*

~ Friedrich Nietzsche

*History is a fairy tale
true to its telling.*

~ Andrei Codrescu

*History teaches
but has no pupils.*

~ Ingeborg Bachmann

*History is hysterical:
it is constituted only if we consider it,
only if we look at it — and in order to look at it,
we must be excluded from it.*

~ Roland Barthes

*Writing, like mourning and history,
designates the place of an irreplaceable,
marks the trace of a disappearance.*

~ Chantal Thomas

Parataxis is more egalitarian ... it's a matter of ceasing to treat things as mere objects to be pushed round by an all-important subject. It means giving things back their autonomy ... Don't ask me, ask the poem. Or rather, let it ask you. If your conversation this afternoon is to lead anywhere, it must be the poem that is guiding us ...

~ Donald Carne-Ross

Literature, to its glory, is a dirty bastard form. From the most vulgar and scurrilous, to the most sublime and poetic. You can put anything in a book, twist it about and turn it into something unforgettable.

~ Hanif Kureishi

IV

Unfettered spaces scare me.
I'm not used to scenes
that aren't in the frame ...
It's probably from all the TV.

~ Izumi Suzuki

All these eejits standing around me, just looking,
staring really, some clearly pretending to care.
Bitch please, I just saw you chuckling to yourself
not quite half a moment after squeezing out that
tear. Shall I pass you an onion for future photo
ops?, will that fake tan it mess up?

Looking out through this box is quite comforting
indeed. That square they place above your face
does screen the world quite nicely indeed.

I squint just so I don't have to see clearly.

Lying there, a memory floats to me, a section from
a poem by Micaela Piñero, « Sorpresa » I believe
she named it:

It would be fair to say I was fairly surprised to find myself in a box.

And when on earth did I start to speak Spanish? *¿a través de una mostacilla?* Can one hear through a bead, listen through a looking glass? Here, I'm almost tempted to say, *only time will tell* ... ratty bastard though she be ...

To know, perchance to dream. One which brings us right to the edge of the river, perhaps even across it, maybe even into its waters. Plunging in — through — Lethe. Once every a while, perhaps someone comes out the other side.

Aletheia.

En mí hay lugar para lo nuevo,

And all I can say is

Gracias gracias gracias gracias gracias
gracias gracias gracias gracias gracias
gracias gracias gracias gracias gracias
gracias gracias gracias gracias gracias
gracias gracias gracias gracias gracias
gracias gracias gracias gracias gracias
a todos y que lluevan laureles
qué lindo que es que lluevan laureles
y todo es tan hermoso
cuando estamos juntos
qué embole que son ellos, ¿no?

Yes, even to you, bitches.

All whilst « looking past a moment into the future », like an echo of Janice Sim would continue to resound ...

*It's goodbye for now
but not forever ...*

~ Mae West

*We'll meet again
some sunny day ...*

~ Vera Lynn

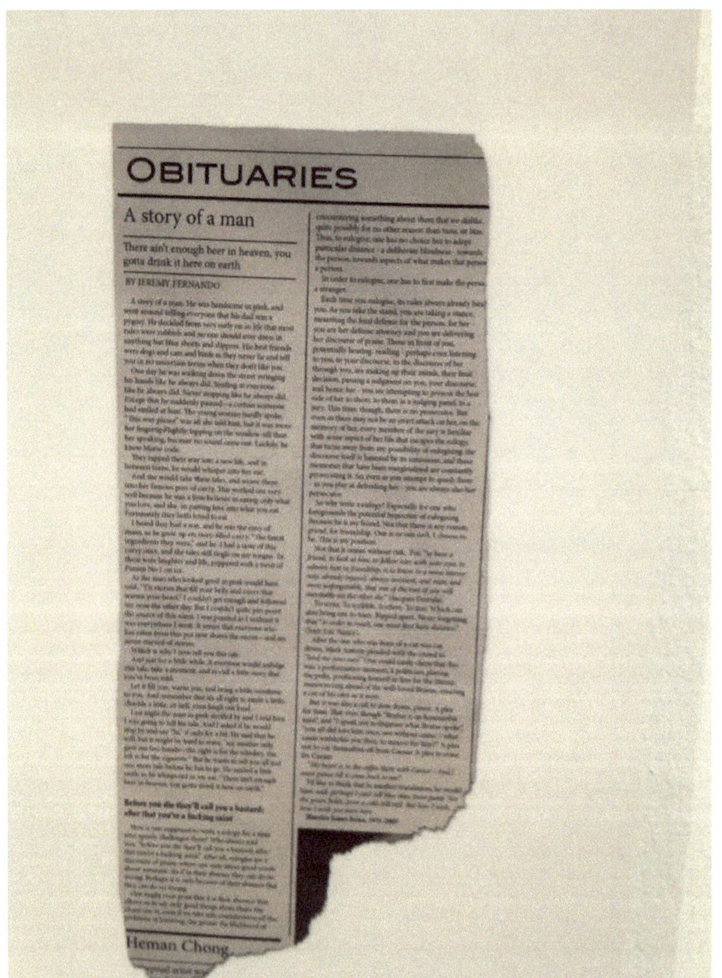

OBITUARIES

A story of a man

There ain't enough beer in heaven, you gotta drink it here on earth

BY JEREMY FERNANDO

Before you die they'll call you a bastard; after that you're a fucking saint

Heman Chong

a story of a man, 2012

Thought, for me, is just that:
the courage of hopelessness.

~ Giorgio Agamben

hills like white elephants, 2018

hoc facite in meam commemorationem, 2017

flower of the sea

From the sea come I, compared to a flower oft been
showing myself after long summer days. Missing me
no lands bloom, much as ingredients turn not into dishes
without first a gentle caress of my hand

The single-most important element
to good cooking is salt

~ Samin Nosrat

Place me in the midst of she not so I become her
but that Salacia find herself in me. Preserve me
not that I become another nor ossify but that
I find myself in me

Bloom

I don't make the soya sauce:
the microorganisms in the air do it.
I just create the right environment
for them to do so

~ Yasuo Yamamoto

Trust no one, Cicero says, *unless you have eaten
much salt with them.* Not as a measure of morality
but that *the salt of any interesting civilisation
is mixture* (Antonio Tabucchi). And coming-together be
where mischief is brewed.

Ideally *much* too.

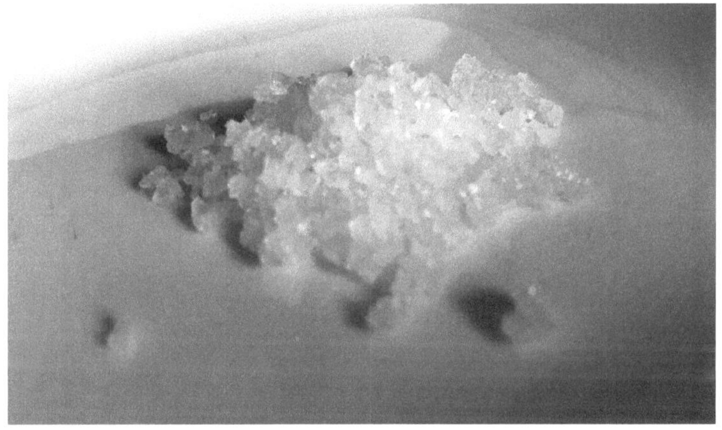

let's drink to the hard-working people / let's drink to the lowly of birth, 2022

As for the shortness of the book I am awfully sorry for it; but what can I do? If you were to squeeze me like a lemon you would get nothing more out of me.

~ Ludwig Wittgenstein

twenty twenty-three

the only thing that
continues to surprise me
is that we are still

surprised that we still
continue to claim to be
surprised each time this

happens as if the
surprise would save us having
to acknowledge that

we would much rather
remain surprised than to not
devour prizes

peoples lands so *this*
is no doubt a perfectly
ordinary year [1]

I wake up in the morning and I wonder
why everything's the same as it was

~ Skeeter Davis [2]

Notes:

[1] closing line to the poem '一九八九年' by Yang Lian, translated into the English as '1989' by Brian Holton.

[2] Sylvia Dee & Arthur Kent, 'The End of the World', single by Skeeter Davis, New York: RCA Victor, 1962.

walls | words, 2018

*It has to be said that writing is an inhuman and
unintelligible activity — one must always do it with a
certain disdain, without illusions, and leave it to others
to believe in one's own work.*

- Jean Baudrillard

Jeremy Fernando reads, writes, and makes things.

He works in the intersections of literature, philosophy, and art; and his, more than thirty, books include *Reading Blindly, Living with Art, Writing Death, in fidelity, Tómate un paseo por el lado oscuro del camino, resisting art, Writing Skin, A Ghost Never Dies, The feather of Ma'at*, and *I wish we were lovers*. His writing has also been featured in magazines and journals such as *Arte al Límite, Berfrois, CTheory, Cenobio, Entropy, Full Bleed, Poiesis, positions, Philosophy World Democracy, Queen Mob's Teahouse, Qui Parle, Testo e Senso, TimeOut*, and *Voice & Verse Poetry Magazine*, amongst others; and has been translated into the Brazilian-Portuguese, French, German, Italian, Japanese, Korean, Spanish, and Serbian. Exploring other media has led him to film, music, and the visual arts; and his work has been exhibited in Seoul, Vienna, Hong Kong, and Singapore. He has been invited to read at the *Akademie der Künste* in Berlin in September 2016; and to deliver a series of performance-readings at the 2018, 2020, and 2022 editions of the *Bienal de la Imagen en Movimiento* in Buenos Aires, the latter at which he also curated a filmic omnibus entitled *reading dreaming malaya*.

He is the general editor of Delere Press; curates the thematic magazine *One Imperative*; is the Jean Baudrillard Fellow at The European Graduate School; co-creator of the private dining experience, People Table Tales; and the writer-in-residence at Appetite, the sensorial laboratory exploring the cross-roads of food, music, and art.

One of my oldest crusades is against the distinction between thought and feeling, which is really the basis of all anti-intellectual views: the heart and the head, thinking and feeling, fantasy and judgment ... and I don't believe it's true ... I have the impression that thinking is a form of feeling and that feeling is a form of thinking.

~ Susan Sontag

I had been writing this book for years, spread out in newspaper columns, without noticing, ignorant of myself as I am, that I was writing my book.

~ Clarice Lispector

*Doesn't art begin
when objects are made intelligent?*

~ Roland Barthes

Neither painting nor drawing, nor art in general, can achieve anything. It is far removed from colonial appetites and does not even wish to beguile one's contemplation: art does not serve and there are no correspondences, intercessions, or contradictions to be found. This painting, this drawing, is entirely autonomous and engrosses the viewer in a vain search for analogies.

~ Hubertus von Amelunxen

www.ingramcontent.com/pod-product-compliance
Lightning Source LLC
Chambersburg PA
CBHW041739300726
48978CB00006B/159